SEEKING YOUR
RELIGION

LARRY CYRIL JENSEN
BRIDGER LEE JENSEN

SEEKING YOUR RELIGION

Larry Cyril Jensen

Bridger Lee Jensen

ISBN: 978-1-971408-14-9 (Paperback)
ISBN: 978-1-971408-15-6 (eBook)

Library of Congress Control Number: 2026904169

Printed in the United States of America

Published by:

info@thequippyquill.com
(302) 295-2278

TABLE OF CONTENTS

INTRODUCTION

This book welcomes you to essentially be the co-author. You will see that every other page belongs to you. In fact, your thoughts, feelings and intentions will be the heart of the book. Here is how this will come about. A short verse or poem will be presented. Both the title of the poem and the poem itself is designed to prompt you to think and feel and to become invested in an important psychological, philosophical, or theoretical concept.

Coming to a better understanding of these topics a/or issues is meant to help you move towards a more joyful and meaningful life. To accomplish this, you are asked to meditate and record your feelings, thinking, and intentions after reading the poems.

However, you may desire a little more information than that provided in a four-line poem. To give you a more clarification and insights an extra source of information is also provided. It comes from Mr. or Mrs. Artificial Information (AI) who were asked to provide and explication of each poem. As you probably know

AI has become a commonly used servant to provide information and opinion based on large amounts of input from established sources in our culture. You may or may not choose to consider AI when drawing your own conclusions but it is there if you want it.

To provide you the convenience for recording your feelings, thoughts and intentions space is provided immediately following the AI explication. Of course, you may also not choose to record your response for every poem but the opportunity will be there and it should provide and opportunity similar to writing in your diary but in this case, you will be writing about very important and serious issues.

Why Choose a Religion?

Always and everywhere, there is religion.

It is a part of life that many depend on.

Some find religion a path to success.

Some find religion brings happiness.

Many uses religion to deal with strife.

Many uses religion to guide their life.

Many choose not to learn about any of this;

Would only a fool choose to know less?

Explication of Poem by Artificial Intelligence

This poem reflects on the enduring presence of religion across human life, portraying it as a universal element that people turn to in different ways. It acknowledges religion's diverse roles: for some, it is a path toward achievement and success; for others, a source of happiness or comfort in times of struggle. The poem also highlights religion's practical function as a guide, offering structure and meaning in daily life. Yet, it doesn't present religion as universally embraced—there are those who choose to remain uninvolved or disinterested, raising the question of whether avoiding knowledge of religion is a deliberate limitation or even a form of foolishness. The tone remains observational rather than prescriptive, neither condemning nor glorifying, but instead suggesting that religion is a force encountered everywhere, shaping individuals differently depending on their orientation toward it. Ultimately, the poem invites reflection on why people engage with or resist religion, and whether ignorance of its influence represents freedom from belief or a missed opportunity for deeper understanding.

Religion, Theology and Spirituality

Religion is not the same as theology
Theology is not the same as spirituality
Yet they live in the same family home,
Each invite for reasons of their own.
It matters not why, when, where or who
It matters not which you like or sit next to
For if hungry and in need of nourishment
Feast at their table and enjoy the moment.

Explication of Poem by Artificial Intelligence

This poem distinguishes between religion, theology, and spirituality, while also emphasizing their shared kinship. It presents the three as distinct yet related—each offering its own purpose and way of engaging with the human search for meaning. Religion is framed as a structured path, theology as the intellectual or doctrinal pursuit, and spirituality as a more personal and experiential dimension. Though different, they are described as living "in the same family home," suggesting that they coexist and interrelate in the broader human experience. The poem minimizes hierarchy or exclusivity, emphasizing that it doesn't matter which one a person gravitates toward, nor the circumstances surrounding that choice. Instead, it suggests a spirit of openness: when in need, one can simply sit at the table of any of these traditions and receive nourishment. The imagery of feasting conveys abundance, hospitality, and the idea that meaning and fulfillment can be found across different approaches. Overall, the poem promotes inclusivity, acceptance, and the recognition that different modes of seeking truth and wisdom ultimately serve the same human hunger.

Choosing a Personalized Religion

In the same church scholars have different religions.

They think and interpret with their own visions.

They value and love their church uniquely.

And with God they speak and hear differently.

God can teach in ways each understands

And with inspiration our thoughts command.

Is this personal religion a step higher?

Is personal religion what God will require?

Explication of Poem by Artificial Intelligence

This poem reflects on the diversity of religious experience even within a shared community. It observes how scholars—or believers more broadly— may belong to the same church yet hold differing interpretations, shaped by their own vision, thought, and personal connection with the divine. The piece acknowledges that each individual values and experiences their faith uniquely, and that dialogue with God is not uniform but personal. Rather than presenting this diversity as a problem, the poem suggests it may reflect God's ability to reach people in ways that are tailored to their understanding. Inspiration, then, becomes an individualized guide that commands thought and devotion. The closing questions turn reflective: is this deeply personal religion—faith shaped by individual relationship rather than strict conformity—perhaps closer to what God truly desires? By raising this possibility, the poem shifts the focus from institutional or collective religion toward an emphasis on personal authenticity and responsiveness in the spiritual life. It invites readers to consider whether individuality in faith is not just acceptable but central to divine intention.

What to Look for in Religion

In past times and in distant places

God was hard and had many faces

But now,

Is God really a heavenly father?

Is God caring and my safe harbor?

Does God hear and answer simple prayers?

Does God comfort me when I have fears?

Do I have here a choice to make?

If so,

The loving God I will take.

Explication of Poem by Artificial Intelligence

This poem explores the evolving human perception of God across time. It contrasts historical images of God—distant, harsh, and manifold—with a more intimate and tender vision emerging in the present. The speaker raises probing questions: is God truly a heavenly father, a caring presence, a safe harbor? Does God listen to simple prayers and provide comfort in fear? These inquiries frame a choice between differing theological and personal interpretations of the divine. Rather than accepting a rigid, inherited image of God, the poem suggests that each individual has agency in shaping their understanding. The final lines reveal the speaker's preference: when given the choice, they embrace the God of love. This conclusion affirms a hopeful, nurturing vision of divinity that prioritizes compassion and relationship over fear and distance. The poem as a whole emphasizes both continuity and change in religious thought, showing how conceptions of God are not static but responsive to human needs, hopes, and experiences across time.

Fitting Religion with Culture

We live in many cultures happily

Including ethnic, school, work, and family.

There are many more than just these few,

And each has a different religious view.

Some cultures are hostile and some kind

But religious truth I alone must find.

Explication of Poem by Artificial Intelligence

This poem considers the interplay between religion and culture, highlighting how people move through many cultural settings—ethnic, educational, professional, and familial, among others. Each of these settings can carry its own religious perspective, shaping how faith is expressed and understood. The tone is realistic, noting that some cultures may be welcoming while others may be hostile, reflecting the variety of experiences individuals face when navigating religious identity in different social contexts. Despite this diversity and potential conflict, the poem emphasizes individual responsibility and agency: ultimately, the search for religious truth is personal. It suggests that while culture influences belief, it does not dictate it, and each person must discern their own understanding. This underscores the autonomy of spiritual discovery, even when cultural forces press in different directions. The poem thus frames religion as something both lived collectively in culture and chosen individually in conscience, pointing to the tension between external context and internal conviction.

How Do We Learn About God?

About God, how do we learn?

First from parent's kind and firm

Then with acquired reason and intellect,

Next, healthy skepticism keeps this in check.

Adulthood allows for the understanding of error--

Error rejected by youth's idealism that all be fair.

But with maturity comes the important learning--

Direct learning from God that is forever ongoing.

Explication of Poem by Artificial Intelligence

This poem traces the stages of learning about God, presenting spiritual understanding as a developmental journey. It begins with childhood, where parents provide the first framework—gentle yet firm guidance that shapes early impressions. As one grows, reason and intellect enter, allowing for critical thinking and a more conscious engagement with inherited beliefs. The poem highlights the value of skepticism, not as rejection but as a balancing force that prevents blind acceptance. In adulthood, disillusionment arises as youthful ideals confront the reality of error and imperfection, both human and institutional. Yet this stage also opens the way for deeper maturity, where the most essential form of knowing emerges: direct, ongoing learning from God. This final insight suggests that true understanding transcends intermediaries—whether parents, intellect, or institutions—and rests in a personal, evolving relationship with the divine. The poem portrays faith as dynamic, shaped by stages of growth, correction, and continual encounter.

Do We Know Everything?

Is my thinking so perverse

To believe only matter

Exists in this universe?

More knowledge can be gathered

More realities detected

When spiritual eyes perfected.

Explication of Poem by Artificial Intelligence

This poem reflects on the boundaries of human understanding and questions whether materialism—the belief that only matter exists—is sufficient to explain the universe. The speaker acknowledges that such a view might appear "perverse," suggesting an awareness of both its dominance in modern thought and its potential limitations. Rather than rejecting materialism outright, the poem invites openness to broader forms of knowledge. It emphasizes that human understanding is progressive: more knowledge can always be gathered, and reality is not exhausted by what has already been discovered. The imagery of "spiritual eyes" points to a deeper way of perceiving, one that goes beyond physical senses or scientific observation. This metaphor suggests that refining spiritual perception can reveal dimensions of reality previously unseen or unacknowledged. The poem thus balances humility and aspiration: it admits that current perspectives may be incomplete while affirming that growth in awareness is possible. Ultimately, it portrays truth as layered and expansive, encouraging a continual search that integrates both intellectual inquiry and spiritual vision.

Personal Religiosity

With so many churches existing

With so many religious teaching

With so many conflicting preaching

With our prayers answered differently

God gives personal religiosity.

Explication of Poem by Artificial Intelligence

This poem centers on the idea of individuality within religious life, presenting "personal religiosity" as a response to the diversity and sometimes conflict within organized faith traditions. It opens by acknowledging the abundance of religious institutions, teachings, and voices that often contradict one another. The sheer number of churches and the variation in preaching highlight the complexity and fragmentation of religion as it is practiced across the world. The poem then shifts to prayer, noting that even when people reach toward the divine in similar ways, the answers they perceive are not uniform. This diversity in response underscores the deeply personal nature of spiritual experience. Rather than suggesting one tradition holds ultimate authority, the poem frames this multiplicity as evidence that God meets individuals where they are, affirming the validity of unique paths. The concept of "personal religiosity" is presented as both a gift and a necessity: a way for individuals to connect authentically with the divine amid competing doctrines. By emphasizing direct, personal experience, the poem highlights the freedom and responsibility of each believer to cultivate their own relationship with God, independent of institutional uniformity.

How Does God Present Truth

Why doesn't God present His truth

In the way we best understand?

God knows science is what we use.

It's the method we demand!

God must think there is a better way.

Could direct knowing be His mainstay?

Direct to our heart, soul, conscience and mind,

His simple truths we directly find.

Explication of Poem by Artificial Intelligence

This poem questions how divine truth is revealed and whether God's methods align with human expectations. It begins with a challenge: if God desires to be known, why not communicate through the language humanity increasingly relies upon—science? The speaker acknowledges that scientific inquiry has become the dominant way of establishing truth in modern culture, a method people "demand" for credibility. Yet the poem suggests that God may choose a different, perhaps superior, approach. Instead of offering truth solely through empirical systems, God may reveal knowledge in a more immediate and personal manner. The second stanza shifts from skepticism to possibility, proposing that God's "mainstay" could be direct communication—truth imparted inwardly to the heart, soul, conscience, and mind. This framing emphasizes simplicity and intimacy, contrasting with the complexity and rigor of scientific proof. Rather than diminishing science, the poem highlights the coexistence of two ways of knowing: one based on external evidence and one rooted in direct experience. Ultimately, it suggests that divine truth is not withheld but may arrive in forms beyond conventional methods, requiring openness to inner perception as a valid channel of understanding.

Spirituality Is Like Singing

Spirituality

And singing are alike

They comfort and excite

They are both beautiful

Joyful and delightful

And to all available.

Explication of Poem by Artificial Intelligence

This poem draws a simple yet evocative comparison between spirituality and singing, presenting both as sources of comfort, joy, and universal accessibility. The imagery suggests that spirituality, like music, is not limited by institutions or boundaries but is something inherently available to everyone. Singing is described as both comforting and exciting—expressions of calm and release alongside energy and passion—and the poem extends these qualities to spirituality. Both are portrayed as beautiful and uplifting experiences that enrich human life. By linking spirituality to something as natural and widely shared as song, the poem emphasizes inclusivity and immediacy: one does not need specialized training, elaborate rituals, or exclusive access to encounter the divine. Instead, spirituality, like music, is woven into human expression and emotion, always present and ready to be engaged. The tone is celebratory and light, underscoring spirituality not as an obligation or heavy doctrine but as something joyful, delightful, and sustaining. Ultimately, the poem affirms that spirituality, like singing, is part of the universal human inheritance—an open, creative, and life-giving practice available to all who choose to engage it.

Matching Personality and Religion

I don't know you

But you do.

I don't know what you are thinking.

Just what in religion are you seeking?

Maybe

Guidance, peace, contentment,

Theology and excitement?

Perhaps

New experiences and feelings,

Familiar teachings and preachings?

Desire first directs what you are seeking

And determines what you will be receiving

Explication of Poem by Artificial Intelligence

This poem considers the deeply personal motivations behind religious engagement, suggesting that what individuals seek in religion often reflects their inner desires and personality. It begins with an acknowledgment of limits: the speaker cannot know another person's thoughts or motivations, only that each individual has their own reasons for approaching faith. The poem then presents possible aims— guidance, peace, contentment, or perhaps intellectual stimulation through theology. It also recognizes that some may pursue excitement, new experiences, or emotional encounters, while others turn to the comfort of familiar teachings and traditions. By listing these varied possibilities, the poem underscores that religion is not a one-size-fits-all experience but adapts to the seeker's needs. The concluding lines propose that desire itself plays a central role: what one looks for in religion shapes what one finds. This dynamic highlights a reciprocal relationship between the seeker and their chosen tradition, where personal orientation influences religious experience as much as religious systems shape the individual. Overall, the poem frames religion less as an external force imposed on people and more as a mirror reflecting the motivations, expectations, and longings each person brings to it.

Does God Intervene in My Personal Life?

How does God run the universe?

Does He bless some and others curse?

Does such a God have time to know me?

Does He my foolish actions see?

Does He from fear and worry set me free

And answer my prayers to give me love?

Could the answer be all of the above?

Surprisingly, it depends on me.

Explication of Poem by Artificial Intelligence

This poem raises questions about divine involvement in both the vast scope of the universe and the intimate details of individual lives. It begins with a cosmic inquiry: if God governs the universe, does that rule include blessing some while cursing others? From there, the focus shifts to a personal level, wondering whether such a God has time to notice an individual, observe their mistakes, or respond to their fears. The questions reflect common struggles of faith—whether God is attentive, compassionate, and responsive to human needs. The poem entertains multiple possibilities, acknowledging that divine action might encompass guidance, liberation from worry, or the granting of love through answered prayers. However, rather than offering a definitive resolution, it concludes with a surprising turn: the degree to which God intervenes may depend on the individual. This suggests that perception, openness, or personal faith shapes how divine presence is experienced. By leaving the responsibility partially with the believer, the poem highlights the interplay between divine potential and human receptivity, framing intervention as both a theological mystery and a personal choice in how one interprets God's role.

Religion and the Family

"Believe in God," his family teaches

And the heart of the boy it reaches.

Oh, the pain when grown--

This precious knowledge is no longer known.

Now, to whom should understanding be shown?

Explication of Poem by Artificial Intelligence

This poem reflects on the formative role of family in shaping religious belief and the challenges that can emerge as children mature. It begins with the image of a boy receiving the teaching, "Believe in God," from his family. The lesson is not presented as abstract instruction but as something that genuinely touches and reaches his heart, suggesting that early faith is often heartfelt, simple, and deeply personal. Yet the tone shifts as the boy grows older. The "precious knowledge" that once felt clear and certain is no longer fully retained or known, symbolizing the struggles of adulthood, where belief may fade, be questioned, or become complicated by life experience. The final line poses a poignant question: if faith is lost or changed, to whom should understanding now be directed? This question leaves the reader in a space of tension, highlighting the difficulty of reconciling childhood teachings with adult realities. The poem does not supply a clear resolution but instead underscores the fragility and evolution of belief, showing how faith within families can inspire, comfort, and also challenge individuals as they grow into independence.

More Truth and Knowledge

Most of us are proud

Our compliments loud

For our wonderful science

And all its accomplishments.

But now please let me know

More than science can show.

Explication of Poem by Artificial Intelligence

This poem reflects on the achievements of science while pointing toward the possibility of truths that lie beyond its reach. It begins by acknowledging humanity's pride in scientific progress and the widespread admiration for its many accomplishments. The tone here is not dismissive but appreciative, recognizing that science has given humanity tools for understanding and shaping the world. Yet, after this affirmation, the poem introduces a deeper question: is science enough? The speaker asks for knowledge beyond what empirical methods can reveal, implying that the scope of human understanding is incomplete if restricted to measurable facts and observable phenomena. By placing this inquiry alongside praise for science, the poem does not set up an opposition but rather a complement—science is celebrated, yet it is not the whole of truth. The concluding request for "more than science can show" opens the door to spiritual, philosophical, or experiential dimensions of knowledge that might address questions science cannot answer. Ultimately, the poem frames human curiosity as expansive and insatiable, suggesting that true wisdom involves both honoring science and remaining open to mysteries that transcend its boundaries.

God's Personality

There is uncertainty

In Christianity

God's personality is described unevenly

His relationship with man stirs controversy.

Is God:

Wrathful?

Merciful?

Demanding?

Or loving?

Distant and cold as a rock?

A caring shepherd of His flock?

A God who loves only a few elect?

A God who loves all and none reject?

A God concerned with only eternal affairs?

A God who answers even a child's small prayer.

Explication of Poem by Artificial Intelligence

This poem explores the complexity and inconsistency of how God is described and understood within Christianity. It begins by acknowledging that God's personality is not presented uniformly, and that His relationship with humanity has long been a source of debate. Through a series of questions, the poem captures the wide spectrum of attributes and portrayals ascribed to the divine. On one side, God may be seen as wrathful, demanding, or distant; on the other, as merciful, loving, and intimately caring for His flock. The tension extends to theological disputes about God's scope of love—whether it is limited to a chosen few or extended universally without rejection. Finally, the poem contrasts views of God's focus: is He primarily concerned with eternal destinies, or is He also attentive to the smallest of human needs, such as the prayer of a child? By presenting these possibilities without resolution, the poem reflects the uncertainty and diversity of interpretation that exists even within a single faith tradition. It highlights how conceptions of God vary across theology, culture, and personal experience, leaving individuals to grapple with competing images and decide for themselves which resonate most deeply.

The Possibility of a
Heavenly Family

The centrality of the family

It is as plain-- as plain can be

Christ prays to a Father in Heaven

Then calls us spiritual children

And the Father calls Him son

After all is said and done.

Most obvious to all is feeling

Male and female deep in our being.

Male and female

What does this tell?

Possibly the reality

Of a heavenly family.

Explication of Poem by Artificial Intelligence

This poem reflects on the theme of family as both a human and divine pattern, suggesting that earthly relationships may mirror a larger, heavenly reality. It begins by emphasizing the centrality of family, describing it as self-evident and foundational. The poem then points to Christian imagery: Christ addressing God as Father, identifying Himself as Son, and calling humanity spiritual children. This language of kinship presents divinity in familial terms, reinforcing the idea of relational connection at the heart of faith. The poem then expands beyond scripture to human experience, noting the "male and female" dynamic felt deeply within human identity and relationships. This natural division and complementarity raise questions about what it might signify in a divine context. The closing lines propose, without claiming certainty, that such patterns could suggest the existence of a heavenly family—a divine structure that parallels and perhaps gives meaning to human family life. Rather than asserting doctrine, the poem presents this as a possibility, encouraging reflection on how human experiences of family, gender, and belonging might point toward larger spiritual truths.

What is the Purpose of Life?

The purpose of life does change dramatically

If I consider time existing endlessly

Short is life compared to all eternity.

God must have eternal reasons for our living

And what better suits His purpose for our being?

Than learning to relate in this mortal place

To become more useful in future time and space.

Explication of Poem by Artificial Intelligence

This poem takes up the timeless question of life's purpose, framing it within the perspective of eternity. It begins with the recognition that our understanding of purpose shifts dramatically if life is viewed not as an isolated span of years but as part of an unending continuum. From this vantage point, earthly existence appears brief, and its meaning must be sought in relation to eternity. The poem proposes that God, who is assumed to have eternal reasons for human existence, provides life as a context for learning. Specifically, it suggests that mortality is a training ground for developing the ability to relate—whether to others, to God, or to the broader dimensions of existence. The final lines point toward a forward-looking vision: by practicing relationships and growth in this world, individuals become better prepared and more "useful" in future realms beyond earthly life. This aligns with themes in many religious and philosophical traditions, where life is seen as preparatory rather than final. Rather than offering definitive answers, the poem opens space for reflection on how present experiences may be part of a larger process of eternal development and purpose.

Is Where We Come From Important?

It seems everybody talks about things heavenly

It seems everybody talks about this mortality

But few talk about a pre-existence reality.

So let me talk of a world before this one

What could have happened in the life we came from?

Spirits would be developing and changing

This then influences what they are now doing

And thus influences where they will be going.

Yes, where I came from is very important

When I consider eternal fulfillment!

Explication of Poem by Artificial Intelligence

This poem turns attention to a dimension of existence often overlooked in mainstream religious discourse: the idea of pre-existence. It begins by noting how much is said about heaven and mortality, yet comparatively little about what may have come before earthly life. The speaker then imagines such a reality, envisioning spirits that developed, changed, and gained experience prior to birth. This vision positions pre-existence not as a vague speculation but as an essential part of the larger story of human purpose. The poem suggests continuity—what happened before shapes present actions, which in turn influence the future. In this way, existence is seen as an ongoing process rather than a series of isolated stages. The conclusion affirms the importance of origins, framing them as central to understanding eternal fulfillment. While this view resonates strongly with traditions such as Latter-day Saint theology, which teaches of a premortal existence, it also connects with philosophical ideas about the soul's prior development found in Plato's writings. Overall, the poem encourages reflection on identity as shaped not only by mortality and eternity but also by what may have preceded both.

What to Know About Injustice

In this world injustice does abound

With unfairness and cruelty all around.

Why does a good God allow this?

The joys of life too many miss.

All explanations fall way short

Unless God's time is made a part

With a pre and post mortality.

Religion offers this reality.

Explication of Poem by Artificial Intelligence

This poem grapples with the enduring question of injustice, asking how a good God can allow cruelty, unfairness, and suffering in the world. It begins by naming the reality: injustice is pervasive, and many people miss the joys of life because of it. The speaker acknowledges that explanations for this dilemma—often framed as the "problem of evil"—fall short if considered only within the limits of earthly time. The turning point comes when eternity is introduced. By viewing life as part of a larger continuum that includes existence before and after mortality, the presence of suffering may take on different meaning. In this framework, injustice is not erased, but it may be contextualized as part of a broader process in which ultimate resolution or fulfillment occurs beyond the present life. The poem closes by noting that religion offers this perspective, providing hope that injustice is not the final word. This echoes many theological traditions that turn to eschatology—the study of ultimate ends—to reconcile the tension between suffering and divine goodness. While not resolving the issue completely, the poem affirms that the lens of eternity offers a way to live with, and find meaning in, the reality of injustice.

God and Different People, Places and Times

It is said that God loves all his children

But then notice

He does not give them the same religion,

Where is the justice?

But I only see this world's place and time,

God must have a world much fairer than mine--

A heaven where all are able God to find.

This path to know God will in the future come

The right religion can tell how this is done.

Explication of Poem by Artificial Intelligence

This poem wrestles with the tension between the belief in God's universal love and the reality of religious diversity. It begins with the assertion that God loves all His children, but then immediately contrasts this with the observation that not everyone is given the same religion. This raises a sharp question of justice: if God loves equally, why are people born into such different spiritual contexts, with access to some teachings but not others? The poem does not dismiss this contradiction but reframes it through the lens of eternity. Earthly life, with its unevenness and limits, is only part of a larger plan. The speaker suggests that in a future existence—a heavenly realm—everyone will have the chance to know God fully and fairly. Religion, in this view, offers guidance by pointing toward that ultimate reconciliation and revealing how such divine justice will be realized. This reflection echoes broader theological discussions about inclusivism and universal access to salvation, found in Christian, Islamic, and even Hindu traditions, where questions arise about how God's justice and mercy extend across cultures and eras. The poem concludes with hope that diversity of belief in this life does not preclude fairness in the life to come.

So Many Religions to Choose

So many religions

They spread confusion

But God doesn't object

When they contradict.

God must have placed in each

Common laws and truths to teach

To love and practice goodness

And treat others with kindness.

So many religions--I'm frustrated in choosing

I trust that in Heaven it won't be confusing

Because for us, God will be there clarifying.

Explication of Poem by Artificial Intelligence

This poem reflects on the bewildering diversity of religions, acknowledging the confusion that arises when faith traditions contradict one another. Rather than framing this as evidence against divine order, the speaker imagines that God does not object to such variety. Instead, the poem suggests that within each religion are shared moral foundations—common truths and guiding principles such as love, goodness, and kindness toward others. These universal values, it implies, may be the real essence that transcends doctrinal differences. Yet the poem also acknowledges the frustration of human choice: faced with so many competing paths, the seeker can feel uncertain about which, if any, represents the full truth. The resolution comes in the hope of heaven, where God Himself will clarify what is now confusing. This assurance points to an eschatological perspective, where ultimate understanding is not found in this life but in the presence of God. The theme resonates with traditions such as perennial philosophy, which holds that diverse religions share a common core, as well as Christian universalism, which looks toward divine reconciliation beyond earthly divisions. In the end, the poem blends realism about human confusion with hope for ultimate clarity and unity in God.

True Freedom is Different

What is true freedom?

"I can do what I want"

That's a mistake upfront.

"I can choose how to act"

Anyone can do that.

"I can freely think"

Here's the missing link:

We are only free

When, with our conscience

We live harmoniously.

Explication of Poem by Artificial Intelligence

This poem questions common assumptions about freedom and redefines it in moral and spiritual terms. It begins by critiquing the notion that freedom simply means doing whatever one wants, calling that view a mistake. It then considers other layers: the ability to choose actions, which is indeed universal, and the capacity to think freely, which the poem identifies as an important but incomplete expression of liberty. The "missing link," it argues, lies in conscience. True freedom emerges not in unrestrained action or thought alone but in living harmoniously with one's moral awareness. This perspective suggests that freedom is not the absence of limits but the alignment of personal will with ethical responsibility. By grounding liberty in conscience, the poem resonates with traditions that connect freedom to virtue—such as Stoic philosophy, which emphasized living in accord with reason, and Christian thought, which often frames freedom as obedience to divine law rather than license. In this view, freedom is less about independence from rules and more about inner integrity. The poem ultimately portrays true freedom as a state of peace and wholeness that arises when choices reflect moral truth I can't remember big Con would you.

Religion With and Without Miracles

Miracles will cause one to believe

And sadly another to disbelieve

Could He just use natural law?

Then everything would be clear to all.

But God has no teaching limitation

So He must have another intention

Instead He must want the following:

Trust and love to overcome doubting,

Belief without forceful convincing

And

For us to learn His way of teaching.

Explication of Poem by Artificial Intelligence

This poem reflects on the ambiguous role of miracles in religious life, observing that while miracles may inspire belief in some, they can just as easily lead others to doubt or reject. The speaker wonders why God does not simply work through natural law in ways that would be universally recognizable, making truth clear and undeniable. Instead, the poem suggests that God's method of teaching is intentional and not bound by human expectations. Miracles, then, are not meant to provide irrefutable proof but to serve a different purpose. The emphasis shifts to trust, love, and the cultivation of faith without coercion. The poem frames belief as something that should not be forced by overwhelming evidence but freely chosen through inner conviction. This interpretation echoes themes in many religious traditions: in Christianity, for example, Jesus sometimes refused to perform signs on demand, emphasizing faith over spectacle; in Buddhism, the focus often lies on practice rather than supernatural displays. The closing lines propose that God's intention is pedagogical—teaching humanity to embrace His ways through a process that engages the heart and conscience, rather than relying solely on dramatic external demonstrations.

Can A Christian Religion Be Bad?

In the quest for power, wealth, pleasure and fame

Men use the words of Christ for personal gain,

Evil and corrupt churches are made in His name.

But the honest and humble this wrong can see

Christ reveals to them God's true reality.

Thus, good and bad churches exist side by side

But which to reject is not hard to decide.

Explication of Poem by Artificial Intelligence

This poem examines the paradox of Christianity's potential for both corruption and authenticity. It begins by acknowledging a painful reality: the words of Christ, meant for love and transformation, have at times been misused by individuals or institutions in pursuit of power, wealth, pleasure, or fame. Such misuse results in churches that may appear outwardly Christian but are inwardly distorted by self-interest and exploitation. Yet the poem does not leave the matter in despair. It affirms that the honest and humble are able to recognize such corruption and see through it to a truer reality. Christ Himself, it suggests, continues to reveal God's truth directly to those who approach faith with sincerity, enabling them to distinguish between genuine and false expressions of religion. The closing lines draw a sharp contrast: both good and bad churches may exist side by side, but the moral difference is clear enough that discerning which to reject is not an impossible task. This reflection echoes broader themes in Christian history and theology, where reform movements have consistently arisen in response to corruption, affirming that divine truth can outlast human misuse.

Relating With God

With God are many ways of being

And also many ways of relating

As a learner

As a pleader

As a worker

As one seeking

As one healing

As one needing

With changing maturity

We relate differently

But there is one finality--

To trust and love openly

Willingly and completely

When He says:

"Come, and I will make you free."

Explication of Poem by Artificial Intelligence

This poem explores the varied ways people connect with God. It begins by noting that there are "many ways of being" with God, followed by a series of roles—learner, pleader, worker, seeker, healer, and one in need. These categories highlight the breadth of human experience, suggesting that people approach God differently depending on their circumstances, emotions, and spiritual stage. The poem then acknowledges that maturity changes how individuals relate, implying that growth in life naturally transforms the way faith is practiced and understood. Yet, amid this diversity, the poem identifies a unifying endpoint: full trust and love. The ultimate form of relationship with God is described as open, willing, and complete surrender, culminating in acceptance of the invitation, "Come, and I will make you free." This conclusion ties personal transformation to divine liberation, emphasizing that freedom arises not through independence but through wholehearted trust. The theme resonates with mystical traditions across religions—whether Christian surrender to God's will, Sufi devotion in Islam, or bhakti (loving devotion) in Hinduism—where love and trust mark the highest form of spiritual union.

Does God Change His Commandments?

In every Christian religion

Commandments have been added

And sometimes deleted.

In every Christian's experience

God at times withdraws

And later with love enthralls.

In every Christian era

God has traditional instructions

And later gives new expectations.

In every life

It is a blessing to have both new and old

Find a changing religion where this truth is told.

Explication of Poem by Artificial Intelligence

This poem reflects on the dynamic character of religious life, particularly within Christianity, and raises the question of whether God's commandments remain fixed or evolve over time. It begins by noting how, across Christian traditions, commandments and practices have been added or removed, illustrating the fluidity of doctrine in different contexts. On a personal level, the poem observes that believers often experience God as both distant and near—sometimes withdrawing, other times returning with love—suggesting that divine interaction itself may feel variable. The historical dimension adds another layer, recognizing that God's instructions in one era may not be identical to those in another, as traditions adapt and new expectations arise. Rather than portraying this variability as contradiction, the poem interprets it as blessing: both continuity and change have value, and together they reveal the richness of faith. The closing lines point to "a changing religion" as the place where such truths are acknowledged, suggesting that spiritual authenticity does not require rigid uniformity but an openness to ongoing revelation. This perspective resonates with traditions that emphasize progressive revelation, as well as broader theological reflections on how timeless principles adapt to cultural and historical circumstances.

Living in This and the Other World

If attention is always on Heaven

Then do we on Earth shirk our work?

Do we lose caring for the living?

Not so my humble observations show

Religion brings more sharing and loving

And opportunities for more serving and giving.

Explication of Poem by Artificial Intelligence

This poem considers the balance between focusing on heaven and living responsibly on earth. It begins with a critical question: if believers keep their attention fixed on the afterlife, does that distract them from their earthly duties, causing them to neglect work or relationships? The concern reflects a common critique of religion—that it can pull people away from the practical demands of daily life. Yet the speaker counters this assumption, offering "humble observations" that religion often inspires greater compassion and engagement rather than withdrawal. Instead of fostering neglect, faith is portrayed as motivating acts of sharing, love, service, and generosity. In this view, belief in heaven enriches earthly life, encouraging responsibility and care for others. The poem affirms that a spiritual orientation toward the afterlife need not conflict with worldly commitments but can strengthen them. This theme resonates with perspectives in many traditions: Christianity, Buddhism, and Islam alike often teach that hope in transcendence leads to ethical action here and now. Ultimately, the poem portrays religion as a bridge between two worlds, reminding believers that devotion to eternal realities should deepen, not diminish, their love and service in the present.

Change, Constancy, and God

Notice, all things change continually

And all the while we seek stability.

We certainly and inevitably change

So why would God's response stay the same?

Reason says God can and will change his mind.

Thus, a changing God be prepared to find.

Explication of Poem by Artificial Intelligence

This poem explores the relationship between human change and divine constancy, questioning whether God must also adapt in response to shifting circumstances. It begins with the observation that everything in life changes—people, relationships, and the world around us. Yet within this constant flux, human beings seek stability, suggesting an innate desire for something enduring. The poem then turns the question back on God: if humanity inevitably changes, can we reasonably expect God's responses to remain the same? From this perspective, a static deity might not be truly responsive to the evolving conditions of creation. Instead, the poem proposes that reason supports the idea of a God who can change His mind, adapting to the realities of human growth and shifting needs. The closing line reinforces this possibility, advising readers to be prepared to encounter a changing God. This interpretation challenges traditional theological claims of divine immutability—held strongly in classical Christianity and philosophy—while aligning more with traditions that emphasize God's relational nature, such as process theology. In doing so, the poem opens space for reflection on whether change in God undermines or deepens divine love, portraying adaptability as a potential expression of care rather than weakness.

Recognizing a Good Religion

How do I find a good religion?

For me this is the central question.

Do I carefully watch the members?

Do I carefully hear the believers?

Are their actions both kind and helpful?

Are their teachings wise and admirable?

If joining would I think more lovingly?

If joining would I become more Godly?

I need not join to know the answer

I need only ask God to know for sure.

Explication of Poem by Artificial Intelligence

This poem reflects on the search for a "good" religion, framing it as one of life's most central questions. It begins by outlining a practical approach: observing members, listening to believers, and evaluating whether their actions align with kindness and their teachings with wisdom. These criteria emphasize that a religion's value is not only in its doctrines but also in the lived character of its community. The poem then turns to self-reflection, asking whether joining would inspire greater love and help an individual grow closer to God. This shifts the standard of evaluation from external observation to internal transformation, suggesting that a good religion should be measured by its capacity to foster moral and spiritual development. Yet the final lines complicate this process of discernment. They affirm that while careful evaluation has its place, ultimate certainty does not come from human judgment alone but from direct appeal to God. This ending emphasizes divine guidance as the highest test of truth, resonating with traditions that prioritize personal revelation, prayer, or conscience as decisive in spiritual matters. In this way, the poem balances reason, observation, and divine confirmation in the pursuit of authentic religion.

A Religion of Hope, a Religion of Love

We would be blind not to see

This life of pain and misery

And with earthly time and space

We resent this human disgrace;

Except when

A religion of hope lets us see past and future time

And shows God will reverse all wrongs we here find.

A religion of love frees us from this mental pain

For focusing on others, we peace of mind obtain.

So

We need not suffer this tragic way

If we live with hope and love each day!

Explication of Poem by Artificial Intelligence

This poem addresses the tension between the harsh realities of human suffering and the transformative potential of religion. It begins by acknowledging the pain, misery, and "disgrace" of earthly existence, reflecting a candid recognition of life's hardships. Yet it quickly turns to religion as a source of vision and resilience. A religion of hope, the poem suggests, allows people to see beyond the limits of time and circumstance, offering confidence that God will ultimately "reverse all wrongs." This hope is not presented as naïve optimism but as a framework for making sense of injustice and maintaining endurance. Complementing hope is love, which provides practical relief from suffering by redirecting attention outward. Through service and care for others, individuals discover peace of mind that mitigates personal pain. The interplay of hope and love thus creates a twofold path: one oriented toward the future promise of divine justice, the other toward present healing through compassion. This vision resonates with Christian theology, where hope and love are often joined with faith as central virtues, but also with broader philosophies that stress altruism as a remedy for despair. Ultimately, the poem portrays hope and love as essential antidotes to life's tragedies.

How Do You Find Spirituality?

Some find God with reason,

Some by experience are drawn,

Others by living God's way of life,

Others experiment to see His light.

Serious study is the way for some

And aging alone brings spiritual wisdom.

God welcomes all regardless of the pathway.

So just pick one and start today.

Explication of Poem by Artificial Intelligence

This poem explores the many pathways through which people discover spirituality, presenting it as a flexible and inclusive journey rather than a rigid formula. It begins by naming reason as one entry point, suggesting that intellectual pursuit and rational inquiry can lead individuals toward God. Experience is highlighted as another path, with direct encounters or feelings drawing some into deeper awareness. Others find spirituality through practice—living in alignment with divine principles—or through experimentation, testing spiritual disciplines to see what brings light. The poem also recognizes study as a valid avenue, where dedicated learning fosters growth, and it honors aging as a natural sand start today"—emphasizing that what matters is not the particular path chosen but the willingness to begin. This inclusive vision resonates with many interfaith perspectives and philosophical traditions that affirm multiple routes to truth. The poem thus frames spirituality as universally accessible, honoring diversity of experience while underscoring the importance of personal commitment.

ABOUT PROFESSOR
LARRY CYRIL JENSEN

Professor Jensen was born in 1938 and grew up in Wyoming, Montana, and Colorado. He is married to Janet and is a father to 10 children, 33 grandchildren, and 3 great-grandchildren.

After graduating from Wheat Ridge High School in Colorado, he received a B.S. and M.S. Degrees from Brigham Young University and his Ph.D. degree from Michigan State University.

Professor Jensen has taught at the following universities:
1. Michigan State University
2. State University of New York at Potsdam
3. Brigham Young University at Provo
4. Brigham Young University at Hawaii
5. Utah State University
6. Southern Virginia University

He has consulted for:
1. Research for Better Schools
2. Journal of Child Development

3. Psychological Reports and Perceptual Motor Skills
4. Family Research Center, Brigham Young University
5. Provo and Salt Lake City Public Schools
6. Institute for Population Studies in Exeter, England

His books include the following:
1. What's Right What's Wrong
2. Understanding and Using Social Influence Techniques
3. That's Not Fair
4. Moral Reasoning: A Philosophical and Psychological Integration
5. Responsibility and Morality
6. Feelings: Helping Children Understand Emotions
7. History of Moral Education
8. Stepping Into Step-Parenting
9. Adolescence
10. Parenting: An Applied Textbook
11. Family Feminism
12. Families: The Key to a Prosperous and Compassionate Society in the 21st Century

He has published multiple scholarly articles in the following journals:

1. Psychological Reports
2. Utah Personnel and Guidance Association Research Bulletin
3. Proceedings of the American Educational Research Association
4. Journal of Educational Psychology
5. Developmental Psychology
6. Journal of Experimental Psychology
7. Journal of Genetic Psychology
8. British Journal of Social and Clinical Psychology
9. Journal of Moral Education
10. Education
11. Educational and Psychological Measurement
12. Psychology in the Schools
13. Sex Roles
14. Journal of Psychology
15. Adolescence
16. International Journal of Social Psychiatry
17. Youth and Society
18. Journal for the Scientific Study of Religion
19. Journal of Business Ethics
20. Family Perspectives
21. Journal of Personality Assessment

22. American Educational Research Journal
23. Addictive Behaviors
24. Journal of Cross-Cultural Psychology
25. Journal of Research and Development in Education
26. Family Therapy
27. Religion and Public Education
28. The Family in America